I'm Dreaming of a
Chocolate Christmas

D1316682

© 2013 by Barbour Publishing, Inc.

Compiled by Cheryl Buskirk in association with Snapdragon Group^{SM}, Tulsa, Oklahoma.

ISBN 978-1-62416-133-9

All scripture quotations are taken from the King James Version of the Bible.

Published by Barbour Publishing, Inc., P.O. Box 719, Uhrichsville, Ohio 44683, www.barbourbooks.com

Our mission is to publish and distribute inspirational products offering exceptional value and biblical encouragement to the masses.

Printed in the United States of America.

— ❄ —

Taste of Christmas

I'm Dreaming of a
Chocolate Christmas

Recipes and Holiday Inspiration for Chocolate Lovers

BARBOUR
PUBLISHING

Every Christmas there are
four things on my list—
dark chocolate, milk chocolate,
white chocolate, and chocolate truffles.

UNKNOWN

Contents

Some things simply go together—churches and steeples, horses and saddles, cups and saucers, and, of course, Christmas and chocolate! After all, gold, frankincense, and myrrh just aren't that tasty. Best case, they can be cashed in to buy more chocolate.

To ensure your Christmas chocolate delight this holiday season, we have collected some of the finest chocolate recipes around—for cakes, pies, cookies, candies, and more. And don't forget, chocolate is always best when it's shared. That's why it goes so well with a hearty helping of Christmas spirit. So go ahead and dream of a "chocolate" Christmas—and enjoy these sweet treats!

When Jesus was born in Bethlehem of
Judaea in the days of Herod the king, behold,
there came wise men from the east to Jerusalem,
saying, Where is he that is born King of the Jews?
for we have seen his star in the east,
and are come to worship him.

MATTHEW 2:1–2

Cakes & Cheesecakes

O Father, may that holy star
Grow every year more bright,
And send its glorious beams afar
To fill the world with light.

WILLIAM CULLEN BRYANT

Winter Warm-Up Hot Lava Cake in a Mug

1 cup all-purpose flour
¾ cup unsweetened cocoa powder
1½ teaspoons baking powder
1 cup brown sugar, packed
1 cup sugar
1 cup salted butter

4 large eggs
1½ teaspoons vanilla extract
¼ teaspoon almond extract
1 (12 ounce) bag semisweet chocolate
   chips
6 mugs

In medium-size bowl, mix flour, cocoa powder, and baking powder, then set aside. In large bowl combine sugars. Melt butter and add to sugar mixture. Mix well with a whisk. Add eggs, one at a time, mixing well. Add vanilla and almond extracts. Mix well. Add dry ingredients and mix well with a whisk. Divide dough evenly into 6 mugs.

Top each one with 2 tablespoons chocolate chips, pressing them down in dough a little with the back of a spoon. Refrigerate lava cups for at least 1 hour before baking. Before baking, take them out of refrigerator and allow to sit at room temperature for 10 minutes. Bake at 350 degrees for 30 minutes. Cakes will appear to "fall" or sink when removed from oven. Allow to cool slightly and serve warm or refrigerate for later. To reheat, place in microwave oven for 15 to 30 seconds.

Yield: 6 servings

Heaven's Delight Chocolate Trifle

1 (18.25 ounce) box devil's food
   cake mix
1 (4.6 ounce) box instant chocolate
   pudding mix

1 (8 ounce) carton whipped topping
1 (6 ounce) package toffee bits

Prepare cake mix as directed; cool, then cut into cubes. Place half the cake cubes in large bowl. Prepare pudding as directed; cool, then pour half of pudding over cake cubes. Cover this with half the whipped topping. Place half the toffee bits on top. Repeat for a second layer. Refrigerate for 2 hours before serving.

Yield: 12 servings

Heavenly Chocolate Caramel Pecan Cake

1 (15.25 ounce) box devil's food
    cake mix
20 caramels, unwrapped
⅓ cup butter or margarine

⅓ cup whipping (heavy) cream
1 cup chopped pecans, toasted
1 (16 ounce) container whipped
    chocolate frosting

Prepare cake mix as directed for two 8- or 9-inch rounds. Cool 10 minutes. Remove from pans to cooling rack. Cool completely. In a saucepan, heat caramels, butter, and whipping cream over medium heat for 6 to 8 minutes, stirring frequently until caramels are melted and mixture is smooth. Stir pecans into melted caramel. Cool 30 to 45 minutes or until firm enough to spread without running over edge of cake. Place one cake layer on plate, round side down. Spread with 1 cup of the pecan filling. Top with second layer, round side up. Spread remaining pecan filling in 4- to 5-inch circle on top of cake. Spread chocolate frosting on sides and around the pecan filling on top. Store loosely covered.

Yield: 12 to 16 servings

Melting Chocolate Christmas Cake

2¼ cups semisweet chocolate chips
1⅔ cups butter
8 eggs, divided

½ cup sugar
1 egg white, beaten until peaks form
½ cup flour

In large bowl, melt chocolate and butter. Set aside. Mix 4 eggs and sugar with whisk. Add flour. Mix well. Add remaining 4 eggs. Blend egg mixture into melted chocolate mixture. Fold in egg white. Pour into 12 ramekins. Bake in preheated, 375-degree oven for about 15 minutes. A crust will form on top, sides, and bottom. The inside will be molten, like pudding.

Yield: 12 servings

Mini Espresso Cheesecakes for Two

2 tablespoons butter
½ cup graham cracker crumbs
2 tablespoons sugar
1 teaspoon instant coffee or
    espresso granules
2 (3 ounce) packages cream cheese,
    softened

⅓ cup sour cream
3 tablespoons sugar
1 large egg
½ cup milk chocolate chips,
    melted and cooled
½ teaspoon vanilla extract

In saucepan, melt butter over medium heat. Remove and stir in graham cracker crumbs, 2 tablespoons sugar, and coffee granules. Press evenly into bottoms of 2 ungreased 4-inch springform pans. Place pans on baking sheet and bake at 350 degrees for 6 to 8 minutes; cool. Reduce oven to 325 degrees. Combine cream cheese, sour cream, and 3 tablespoons sugar. Beat at medium speed with electric mixer until blended. Add egg, beating just until blended. Stir in melted chocolate and vanilla. Pour filling into pans. Bake for 21 to 23 minutes or just until set. Chill until ready to serve.

Yield: 2 servings

Christmas Mocha Melt

½ cup butter, melted
1 cup sugar
½ cup all-purpose flour
2 large eggs, lightly beaten
3 tablespoons cocoa

2 tablespoons finely chopped pecans
1 teaspoon instant coffee granules
½ teaspoon ground cinnamon
1 teaspoon vanilla extract

Mix all ingredients in medium bowl, stirring until blended. Pour into greased 8-inch baking dish (mixture will be shallow in dish). Bake, uncovered, at 325 degrees for 25 minutes. Serve with coffee-flavored ice cream.

Yield: 6 servings

Very Merry Chocolate Cake

1 (15.2 ounce) box devil's food
   cake mix
1 (3.4 ounce) package instant
   chocolate pudding mix
1 (8 ounce) carton sour cream
½ cup oil

½ cup lukewarm water
4 large eggs
1½ cups semisweet chocolate chips
2 tablespoons powdered sugar
Whipped topping or ice cream

In large bowl, blend cake mix, pudding mix, sour cream, oil, water, and eggs.
Beat 5 minutes with electric mixer at medium speed. Stir in chocolate pieces.
Pour into well-greased and floured Bundt or tube pan. Bake at 350 degrees for
approximately 1 hour or until done. Cool 15 minutes on wire rack. Remove
from pan and cool completely. Sprinkle with powdered sugar. Top with
whipped topping or ice cream.

Yield: 12 servings

Chocolate Cheesecake

Crust Ingredients:

1¼ cups graham cracker crumbs

¼ cup sugar

5 tablespoons butter, melted

Filling Ingredients:

1 (6 ounce) package semisweet real chocolate chips

3 (8 ounce) packages cream cheese, softened

½ cup sugar

2 eggs

1 cup heavy cream

⅓ cup hot water

1 teaspoon vanilla extract

1 (12 ounce) jar caramel ice-cream topping, warmed

In small bowl, mix graham cracker crumbs and sugar. Add butter, blending well. Press crumb mixture onto bottom and partly up sides of well-greased 8-inch springform pan. Smooth crumb mixture along bottom to even thickness. Melt chocolate in top of double boiler over hot water. Set aside. In large bowl, beat together cream cheese and sugar until light. Add eggs, one at a time, beating well after each addition. Beat in heavy cream. Pour melted chocolate slowly into cheese mixture. Add hot water and vanilla to cheese mixture. Mix ingredients thoroughly. Pour mixture into prepared crust. Bake at 350 degrees for 45 minutes or until edges of cake are puffed slightly. Turn off oven and allow cake to cool in oven for about 1 hour. Remove from oven; cool to room temperature. Chill. Drizzle with caramel topping just before serving.

Yield: 10 to 12 servings

Merry Christmas Malt Cake

Cake Ingredients:

½ cup butter, softened
1 cup sugar
4 large eggs
1 teaspoon vanilla extract

1 cup all-purpose flour
2 tablespoons malted milk powder
½ teaspoon salt
½ teaspoon chocolate syrup

Frosting Ingredients:

½ cup butter or margarine, softened
2 cups powdered sugar

1 teaspoon malted milk powder
Milk

Topping Ingredients:

1 cup semisweet chocolate chips
¼ cup butter or margarine

1½ cups chopped malted milk balls
(frozen and chopped with food
chopper)

Cake preparation: Beat butter at medium speed until creamy. Add sugar, beating well. Add eggs and vanilla; beat well. Combine flour, 2 tablespoons malted milk powder, and salt. Add to butter mixture, beating well. Stir in chocolate syrup. Pour batter into greased 13 x 9-inch pan. Bake at 350 degrees for 28 minutes. Cool completely. Frosting preparation: Beat butter at medium speed until creamy. Add powdered sugar and 1 teaspoon malted milk powder, beating until smooth. Add small amounts of milk until proper spreading consistency is reached. Spread frosting over cake. Topping preparation: Combine chocolate chips and butter in small saucepan. Cook over low heat until chocolate and butter are melted, stirring often. Cool 5 minutes. Spread over frosted cake. Sprinkle with chopped malted milk balls, pressing gently into frosting and topping. Cover and chill 1 hour before serving.

Yield: 12 servings

Double-Chocolate Praline Christmas Cake

Cake Ingredients:

1 cup butter
¼ cup cocoa
1 cup water
½ cup buttermilk
2 large eggs

1 teaspoon baking soda
1 teaspoon vanilla extract
2 cups sugar
2 cups all-purpose flour
½ teaspoon salt

Chocolate Ganache Ingredients:

2 cups (12 ounces) semisweet
  chocolate chips

⅓ cup whipping cream
¼ cup butter, cut into pieces

Praline Frosting Ingredients:

¼ cup butter or margarine
1 cup light brown sugar, packed
⅓ cup whipping cream

1 cup powdered sugar
1 teaspoon vanilla extract
1 cup chopped pecans, toasted

In saucepan, melt butter, cocoa, and water over low heat, stirring constantly until smooth. Set aside to cool. In bowl, beat buttermilk, eggs, baking soda, and vanilla at medium speed until smooth. Add butter mixture to buttermilk mixture, beating until blended. (Batter should be thin.) Spray 3 (8-inch) round cake pans with cooking spray and line with waxed paper. Pour batter into pans, and bake at 350 degrees for 22 to 24 minutes or until set. Cool in pans for 10 minutes. Remove from pans and cool completely. To prepare ganache, microwave chocolate chips and cream in glass bowl at 50 percent power for 2 to 3 minutes. Whisk until smooth. Cool, whisking often, until proper spreading consistency (15 to 20 minutes). Stack 3 cooled cakes, spreading ½ cup of ganache between each cake layer and remainder of ganache on sides of cake. Chill for 30 minutes. To prepare praline frosting, boil butter, brown sugar, and cream together in 2-quart saucepan over medium heat for about 1 minute, stirring often. Remove from heat. Whisk in powdered sugar and vanilla until smooth. Add toasted pecans. Stir gently for 2 to 5 minutes or until frosting begins to cool and thicken. Immediately pour frosting slowly over center of cake; spread to edges, allowing some to run over sides.

Yield: 8 to 10 servings

Magi Candy Bar Cake

Ingredients for Mixture #1:
½ cup butter
1 cup sugar

1 cup brown sugar

Ingredients for Mixture #2:
1 cup frozen, crushed chocolate-
    covered toffee candy bars

½ cup chopped pecans or almonds

Ingredients for Mixture #3:
2 cups all-purpose flour
1 teaspoon baking soda
½ teaspoon salt

1 teaspoon vanilla extract
1 cup buttermilk
1 large or 2 small eggs

Cream together ingredients for Mixture #1. Reserve 1 cup to be used later. In separate bowl, combine the ingredients for Mixture #3. Add to Mixture #1. Pour into 9 x 13-inch baking pan. Combine ingredients for Mixture #2 and add reserved cup from Mixture #1. Pat this crumb mixture on top of batter. Bake at 350 degrees for 25 to 30 minutes.

Yield: 12 servings

White Chocolate Fudge Cake

Cake Ingredients:

1 (18.25 ounce) box white cake mix

1 (3 ounce) white chocolate baking bar, vanilla-flavored candy coating, or almond bark, chopped, then melted

Fudge Filling Ingredients:

1 cup semisweet chocolate chips

3 tablespoons margarine or butter

2 tablespoons light corn syrup

¼ cup powdered sugar

Frosting Ingredients:

1 (16 ounce) container prepared vanilla frosting

1 (3 ounce) white chocolate baking bar, vanilla-flavored candy coating, or almond bark, chopped, then melted

1 teaspoon vanilla extract

1 (8 ounce) container frozen whipped topping

Garnish Ingredients:

Chocolate curls

Prepare cake mix as directed on box. Before pouring into pan, gradually beat in melted white chocolate until well blended. Pour batter into greased and floured 13 x 9-inch pan. Bake at 350 degrees for 25 to 35 minutes. Cool 10 minutes. In small saucepan, combine chocolate chips and margarine. Stir over low heat until melted. Stir in corn syrup and powdered sugar until well blended. Spread fudge filling over warm cake. Cool completely. In large bowl, beat frosting at medium speed, gradually adding melted white chocolate. Beat at high speed 30 seconds or until smooth and well blended. Fold in vanilla and whipped topping. Refrigerate. Frost cake and garnish with chocolate curls. Store in refrigerator. Let stand at room temperature for 10 minutes before serving.

Yield: 15 servings

Chocolate Candy Cheesecake

Crust Ingredients:

11 chocolate sandwich cookies with white cream filling, crushed

3 tablespoons butter, melted

Filling Ingredients:

24 ounces cream cheese
⅓ cup dark brown sugar
¼ cup dark corn syrup
5 teaspoons cornstarch
3 eggs
1 egg yolk

1 cup semisweet chocolate chips, melted
⅓ cup whipping cream
2 teaspoons vanilla extract
1 cup white chocolate chips, melted

Creamy Chocolate Topping Ingredients:

3 tablespoons butter
2 cups sifted powdered sugar
¼ cup unsweetened cocoa powder

1 teaspoon vanilla extract
1 teaspoon milk
Small chocolate candies

In small bowl, stir together crushed cookies and melted butter until well combined. Press crumb mixture evenly onto bottom of greased 9-inch springform pan. In large bowl, combine cream cheese, brown sugar, corn syrup, and cornstarch. Beat with electric mixer until smooth. Add eggs and egg yolk, one at a time, beating well after each addition. Stir in melted chocolate, whipping cream, and vanilla extract. Stir in melted white chocolate. Pour cream cheese mixture over crust. Bake at 350 degrees for 15 minutes. Lower temperature to 200 degrees and bake for 80 to 90 minutes, or until center no longer looks shiny. Remove from oven and run a knife around inside edge of pan. Chill, uncovered, overnight. In small mixing bowl, beat butter until smooth. Gradually add 1 cup powdered sugar and cocoa powder. Beat well. Slowly beat in vanilla and milk. Add remaining powdered sugar and beat until smooth. Add more milk, if necessary, for better consistency. Spread mixture over cheesecake. Garnish with chocolate candies. Chill until serving time.

Yield: 8 to 10 slices

Cinnamon Chocolate Cake

Cake Ingredients:

2 cups all-purpose flour
2 cups sugar
1½ teaspoons ground cinnamon
¼ teaspoon salt
1 cup water
½ cup vegetable oil

½ cup butter
¼ cup cocoa powder
2 eggs
½ cup buttermilk
1 teaspoon vanilla extract
1 teaspoon baking soda

Frosting Ingredients:

½ cup butter
⅓ cup whipping cream
¼ cup cocoa powder
1½ teaspoons ground cinnamon

3 cups powdered sugar
1 teaspoon vanilla extract
1 cup chopped pecans or walnuts

In large mixing bowl, combine flour, sugar, cinnamon, and salt; set aside. In saucepan, combine water, oil, butter, and cocoa, and bring to a boil over medium heat. Pour over dry ingredients; mix well. Add eggs, buttermilk, vanilla, and baking soda, and mix well. Pour into greased and floured 15 x 10 x 1-inch baking pan. Bake at 375 degrees for 15 to 20 minutes. Combine butter, cream, and cocoa for frosting. Stir over medium heat until butter is melted and mixture is heated through. Remove from heat; beat in cinnamon, sugar, and vanilla until smooth. Carefully spread over hot cake. Sprinkle with nuts.

Yield: 24 to 30 servings

Cherry-Chocolate Fudge Bundt Cake

Cake Ingredients:
1 (18.25 ounce) box dark fudge cake mix
3 eggs
1 (21 ounce) can cherry pie filling

¼ cup cooking oil
1 teaspoon almond extract

Icing Ingredients:
1 tablespoon butter
½ cup semisweet chocolate chips
½ cup powdered sugar

1 tablespoon milk
Maraschino cherries

In large bowl, combine cake mix, eggs, pie filling, oil, and extract by hand, working to keep cherries from breaking up too much. Batter will be thick and fluffy. Pour into prepared Bundt pan. Bake at 350 degrees for 1 hour or until center seems firm and is barely pulling away from sides. Remove and cool until it is cool enough to turn onto plate. In saucepan, melt butter and chocolate chips. Add sugar. Mix well. Stir milk into hot mixture. Add tiny drops of very hot water to thin if needed. Drizzle over cooled cake. Decorate with maraschino cherries.

Yield: 12 servings

Holiday Upside-Down German Chocolate Cake

1½ cups chopped pecans
1 cup coconut
1 (18.25 ounce) box German
   chocolate cake mix

1 (8 ounce) package cream cheese
½ cup margarine
1 (1 pound) package powdered sugar

Spread chopped pecans and coconut evenly in bottom of greased and floured 13 x 9-inch pan. Prepare cake mix according to directions on box. Pour batter evenly over nuts and coconut. To prepare topping, whip cream cheese, margarine, and sugar with electric mixer until smooth. Pour evenly over top of cake mixture. Bake at 300 degrees for 1 to 1½ hours. Cool in pan. Can be served from baking dish or turned onto a serving dish.

Yield: 12 to 20 servings

Aunt Emma Jean's Holiday Turtle Cake

Cake Ingredients:

1 (18.25 ounce) box German
  chocolate cake mix
1 (14 ounce) package caramels
¼ cup evaporated milk

¾ cup melted butter or margarine
1 (12 ounce) bag semisweet chocolate
  chips
1½ cups chopped pecans

Frosting Ingredients:

½ cup butter or margarine
2 tablespoons cocoa powder
6 tablespoons evaporated milk

1 (16 ounce) box powdered sugar
1 teaspoon vanilla extract
1 cup chopped pecans (optional)

Prepare cake mix as directed. Pour half the batter into greased and floured 13 x 9-inch pan. Bake at 350 degrees for 12 to 15 minutes. While cake is baking, melt caramels in saucepan with evaporated milk and butter. Blend well. Remove cake from oven, and pour caramel mixture over top. Sprinkle chocolate chips and nuts over caramel mixture. Pour remaining batter over cake. Bake 20 minutes or longer if needed. Cool completely. Mix butter, cocoa, and evaporated milk in saucepan over low heat; add sugar and vanilla. Spread over cake. Sprinkle with pecans.

Yield: 12 to 15 servings

Black Forest Holiday Cake

1 (18.25 ounce) box devil's food *or* chocolate fudge cake mix

1 (21 ounce) can cherry pie filing

½ (8 ounce) container frozen whipped topping, thawed

Prepare cake mix as directed and bake using 2 round cake pans. Cool completely. Place one cake on cake plate, top side down. Spread half the cherry pie filling on the top only. Add second cake, flat side down. Frost cake sides with frozen whipped topping. Spoon remaining cherry pie filling on top of cake. Store in refrigerator until ready to serve.

Yield: 8 to 10 servings

German Holiday Cake

½ cup butter, melted
1 cup pecans
1 cup coconut
1 (18.25 ounce) box German
chocolate cake mix

1 (8 ounce) package cream cheese
½ cup butter
1 teaspoon vanilla extract
1 (1 pound) package powdered sugar
1½ cups milk chocolate chips

Pour melted butter into bottom of 9 x 13-inch baking pan. Sprinkle pecans and coconut over butter. Prepare cake mix as directed and pour batter over first layer of ingredients. Melt cream cheese, butter, vanilla, and sugar together and spoon over top of cake mixture. Sprinkle chocolate chips over top. Bake at 350 degrees for 50 to 60 minutes.

Yield: 12 to 14 servings

Joy's Triple-Chocolate Mousse Cake

½ cup chocolate syrup
1 (18.25 ounce) box chocolate cake mix
1 cup water
⅓ cup oil
7 eggs, divided
½ cup sour cream
1 (8 ounce) package cream cheese, softened

1 cup sugar
1 (12 ounce) can evaporated milk
4 (1 ounce) squares semisweet chocolate, melted
1 cup frozen nondairy whipped topping, thawed

Pour chocolate syrup into 12-cup fluted pan sprayed with cooking spray. Beat cake mix, water, oil, and 3 eggs with mixer for 2 minutes on medium speed. Add sour cream. Mix well. Pour over syrup in pan. Beat cream cheese and sugar until blended. Add remaining eggs, mixing well. Blend in evaporated milk and melted chocolate. Gently spoon over cake batter in pan. Cover with foil sprayed with cooking spray, sprayed-side down. Place fluted pan in a shallow pan. Add enough water to come at least 2 inches up the side of the fluted pan. Bake at 375 degrees for 90 minutes. Cool cake completely in pan. Refrigerate 2 hours. Invert cake onto plate. Serve cake topped with whipped topping.

Yield: 24 servings

Pies & Cobblers

When we recall Christmas past, we usually find
that the simplest things—not the great occasions—
give off the greatest glow of happiness.

BOB HOPE

Wintry White Chocolate-Mint Pie

3 (4 ounce) white chocolate bars, divided
2 large eggs, beaten
⅓ cup powdered sugar
1¾ cups heavy whipping cream, divided

2 to 3 teaspoons peppermint extract
1 teaspoon vanilla extract
1 (6 ounce) chocolate crumb piecrust
8 chocolate wafer cookies

Melt 2 chocolate bars in double boiler, stirring often. In bowl, stir a small amount of chocolate into beaten eggs. Add remaining chocolate, stirring constantly. Stir in powdered sugar and ¼ cup whipping cream until smooth. Cook over medium heat, stirring constantly, until candy thermometer registers 160 degrees. Remove from heat; cool, stirring constantly. Add extracts. Beat remaining 1½ cups whipping cream at high speed with an electric mixer until stiff peaks form. Gently fold whipped cream into chocolate. Spoon filling into crust, mounding in center.

Break 6 wafer cookies in half. Finely crush remaining 2 cookies; sprinkle crumbs over pie. Shave edges of remaining chocolate bar with vegetable peeler to make white chocolate curls. Sprinkle curls over pie. Cover and freeze pie at least 8 hours.

Yield: 8 servings

Grandma's Fudge Pie

½ cup butter or margarine
1 cup sugar
½ cup all-purpose flour
2 eggs

1 teaspoon vanilla extract
2 tablespoons cocoa powder
1 (9 inch) piecrust

Melt butter; cream sugar into it. Add remaining ingredients, except piecrust. Mix well. Pour into piecrust. Bake at 325 degrees for 25 to 30 minutes.

Yield: 8 to 10 servings

Dreamy Chocolate Christmas Cobbler

Filling Ingredients:

¾ cup sugar

1 cup self-rising flour

2 tablespoons cocoa powder

½ cup milk

3 tablespoons butter, melted

1 teaspoon vanilla extract

Topping Ingredients:

½ cup sugar

½ cup brown sugar

¼ cup cocoa powder

1½ cups hot water

In large bowl, mix filling ingredients together and spread into greased 11 × 7-inch glass baking dish. Mix together all topping ingredients, except water, and sprinkle evenly on top. Pour hot water gently over all. *Do not mix.* Bake at 350 degrees for 40 minutes. Serve hot or cold.

Yield: Approximately 12 to 15 servings

Santa's Chocolate Meringue Pie

Filling Ingredients:

½ cup cocoa powder
1½ cups sugar
¼ cup cornstarch or flour
¼ teaspoon salt

3 egg yolks
2 cups milk
1 (9 inch) baked pie shell

Meringue Ingredients:

3 egg whites

4 tablespoons brown sugar

In large bowl, mix cocoa, sugar, cornstarch, and salt. Add egg yolks and milk. Cook mixture in double boiler until thick, stirring constantly. Pour into baked pie shell. Prepare meringue by beating egg whites until peaks form. Add brown sugar. Spread over pie and bake at 400 degrees until meringue turns slightly brown.

Yield: 8 servings

Cream Cheese Brownie Pie

1 (8 ounce) package cream cheese
3 tablespoons sugar
1 teaspoon vanilla extract
3 eggs, divided
1 (15.1 ounce) package brownie mix

¼ cup oil
2 tablespoons water, divided
1 (9 inch) refrigerated piecrust
½ cup chopped pecans
½ cup hot fudge ice-cream topping

In medium bowl, combine cream cheese, sugar, vanilla, and 1 egg. Beat until smooth and set aside. In large bowl, combine brownie mix, oil, 1 tablespoon water, and remaining 2 eggs. Beat 50 strokes with a spoon. Spread ½ cup of brownie mixture in bottom of piecrust. Carefully spread cream cheese mixture over brownie layer. Top with remaining brownie mixture; spread evenly. Sprinkle with pecans. Bake at 350 degrees for 40 to 50 minutes or until center is puffed and crust is golden brown. Place hot fudge in microwaveable bowl. Microwave at 100 percent for 30 seconds. Stir in remaining tablespoon water. Drizzle fudge over top of pie. Cool 3 hours. Store in refrigerator.

Yield: 8 servings

Chocolate Sandwich Cookie Dessert

24 chocolate sandwich cookies with white cream centers
1 cup butter or margarine, divided
½ gallon vanilla ice cream
1 (4 ounce) German chocolate bar
⅔ cup sugar

⅔ cup evaporated milk
1 teaspoon vanilla extract
⅛ teaspoon salt
1 (16 ounce) container whipped topping
1 cup pecans, chopped

Crush cookies in blender. Spread in 13 x 9-inch baking dish. Melt ½ cup butter and pour over crushed cookies. Let cool. Cut ice cream into ½-inch slices and place on top of cookies. Put in freezer for 30 to 40 minutes. Meanwhile, in saucepan, bring remaining ½ cup butter, chocolate bar, sugar, evaporated milk, vanilla, and salt to a boil. Boil 4 minutes. Cool completely. Pour over ice cream. Refreeze until firm. Spread whipped topping on top. Sprinkle pecans over all. Keep frozen.

Yield: 12 servings

Christmas Turtle Dessert

24 ice-cream sandwiches, divided
1 (12.25 ounce) jar caramel topping
2 cups chopped pecans, toasted, divided

1 (12 ounce) container whipped topping, thawed
¾ cup hot fudge topping, heated

Place 12 ice-cream sandwiches in 13 x 9-inch baking dish. Spread evenly with caramel topping, and sprinkle with 1½ cups pecans. Top with 2 cups whipped topping and remaining ice-cream sandwiches. Sprinkle with remaining ½ cup pecans. Cover and freeze at least 2 hours. Let stand 5 minutes before serving; cut into squares. Drizzle with fudge topping.

Yield: 12 servings

Walnut Fudge Pie

Pie Ingredients:
½ cup brown sugar, firmly packed
¼ cup all-purpose flour
¼ cup butter or margarine, melted
1 teaspoon vanilla extract
3 large eggs, lightly beaten

2 cups semisweet chocolate chips, melted
1½ cups walnut halves
1 (9 inch) piecrust
Coffee ice cream

Fudge Sauce Ingredients:
1 (6 ounce) package semisweet chocolate chips
½ tablespoon butter or margarine

¼ cup whipping cream
2 tablespoons strong brewed coffee

In large bowl, combine first 5 ingredients, stirring until blended. Stir in melted chocolate chips and walnuts. Spoon filling into piecrust. Bake at 375 degrees for 30 minutes. Cool completely on wire rack. Prepare fudge sauce by placing chocolate chips and butter in heavy saucepan. Cook over low heat until chocolate and butter melt, stirring often. Gradually whisk in cream. Cook, stirring constantly, for 2 to 3 minutes or until smooth. Remove from heat; stir in coffee. Serve pie with ice cream and warm fudge sauce.

Yield: 8 to 10 servings

Christmas Brownie Trifle

1 (19.9 ounce) box brownie mix
2½ cups cold milk
1 (3.4 ounce) package instant
  cheesecake pudding mix

1 (3.4 ounce) package instant white
  chocolate pudding mix
1 (8 ounce) container whipped
  topping
2 to 3 butter-toffee candy bars,
  chopped

Prepare brownies as directed for cakelike brownies using 13 x 9-inch pan.
Remove from oven and let cool for 30 minutes. Beat milk and pudding mixes
on low speed for 2 minutes. Fold in whipped topping. Cut brownies into
1-inch squares. Place half in bottom of a bowl. Cover with half of pudding
mixture. Repeat layers and sprinkle with chopped toffee bars. Refrigerate
leftovers.

Yield: 12 to 15 servings

Mama's Festive Black Bottom Pecan Pie

2 eggs, slightly beaten
1 cup sugar
½ cup all-purpose flour
½ cup butter, melted and cooled
1 cup chopped pecans

1 (6 ounce) package semisweet
   chocolate chips
1 teaspoon vanilla extract
1 unbaked 9-inch pastry shell

Combine eggs, sugar, flour, and butter in medium mixing bowl and beat with electric mixer just until blended. Stir in pecans, chocolate chips, and vanilla. Pour filling into pastry shell and bake at 350 degrees for 45 to 50 minutes. Cool completely before serving.

Yield: 8 to 10 servings

Cinnamon Fudge Mocha Pie

½ cup butter

1 tablespoon instant coffee granules

4 (1 ounce) unsweetened chocolate squares

3 large eggs

1 cup sugar

1 teaspoon vanilla extract

⅓ cup all-purpose flour

1 tablespoon ground cinnamon

1 (9 inch) deep-dish pastry shell

Caramel topping, as desired, warmed

1 (8 ounce) container unsweetened whipped topping

Ground cinnamon, as desired

In saucepan, melt butter over medium-low heat. Stir in coffee granules. Add chocolate, stirring until melted. Remove from heat to cool. In bowl, beat eggs with a wire whisk, then gradually beat in sugar. Slowly stir in cooled melted chocolate mixture and vanilla. Add flour and 1 tablespoon cinnamon. Pour filling into pie shell. Bake at 350 degrees for 25 minutes or until set. Serve slightly warm or at room temperature with caramel topping, whipped topping, and cinnamon.

Yield: 8 servings

Holiday Special Chocolate Pecan Pie

4 large eggs
6 tablespoons butter
½ cup sugar
¼ cup light brown sugar
1 cup light corn syrup
1 tablespoon all-purpose flour

1 tablespoon vanilla extract
1 cup coarsely chopped pecans
1 cup (6 ounces) semisweet chocolate
   chips, melted
1 (9 inch) piecrust

In large bowl, whisk eggs, then add the following 6 ingredients until blended.
Stir in pecans and melted chocolate. Pour filling into piecrust. Bake on lowest
rack in oven at 350 degrees for 1 hour or until set, shielding pie with aluminum
foil after 20 minutes. Let pie cool completely on wire rack.

Yield: 8 servings

Crunchy "Choco-licious" Ice Box Pie

¾ cup whole milk
¾ cup semisweet chocolate chips
¼ cup cold water
2 tablespoons cornstarch
1 (14 ounce) can sweetened
   condensed milk
3 large eggs, beaten

1 teaspoon vanilla extract
3 tablespoons butter, unsalted
1 (9 inch) graham cracker crust
Whipped topping
½ cup chopped pecans
1 (1.5 ounce) milk chocolate bar,
   chopped into small pieces

Heat milk over medium heat in 3-quart saucepan. Do not boil. Remove from heat and stir in chocolate chips until melted. Cool slightly. While cooling, stir together water and cornstarch in a cup until cornstarch is fully dissolved. Add cornstarch mixture, condensed milk, eggs, and vanilla to chocolate mixture. Whisk constantly while bringing mixture to a boil. Boil 1 minute or until mixture thickens. Remove from heat, and whisk in butter. Pour mixture into piecrust and spread evenly. Cover and chill in freezer for 8 hours. Remove and spread liberally with whipped topping. Sprinkle with pecans and chocolate pieces.

Yield: 8 servings

Mary's Mint-Chocolate Mousse Pie

1 (11.1 ounce) package no-bake
    cheesecake
5 tablespoons butter, melted
2 tablespoons sugar
1 cup milk
½ cup chocolate-mint flavored syrup

2 (1.55 ounce) minty milk chocolate
    bars with crunchy cookie bits, finely
    chopped
Whipped topping, canned
Chopped chocolate bars

Prepare graham cracker crust according to package directions for no-bake
cheesecake. Press firmly into 9-inch pie pan. In medium bowl, combine milk
and chocolate-mint syrup. Stir well. Add cheesecake filling mix from package
and blend at low speed until thoroughly mixed. Beat an additional 3 minutes at
medium speed. Fold in finely chopped chocolate. Spoon chocolate mixture into
prepared crust. Cover and chill at least 1 hour. Garnish with whipped cream
swirls. Sprinkle chopped chocolate bits on top.

Yield: 8 servings

Rich & Delicious Chocolate Cream Pie

Filling Ingredients:

1 (5.9 ounce) package instant
  chocolate pudding mix
¼ cup cocoa powder
1¼ cups half-and-half

1 cup milk
1 teaspoon vanilla extract
1 (9 inch) pie shell, baked and cooled

Topping Ingredients:

2 tablespoons plus 1 teaspoon water
2 tablespoons sugar
1 teaspoon unflavored gelatin

1 cup heavy whipping cream
Cocoa powder for dusting

In large bowl, combine pudding mix, cocoa powder, half-and-half, milk, and vanilla. Whisk 2 to 3 minutes and pour into piecrust. Refrigerate. Combine water, sugar, and unflavored gelatin in small saucepan. Melt over low heat for 3 minutes. Cool slightly. Whip cream in electric mixer until frothy. While beating, add gelatin mixture in a thin stream. Beat until stiff peaks form. Spread over chocolate filling and dust with cocoa powder. Refrigerate at least 1 hour before serving.

Yield: 8 servings

Christmas French Silk Pie

1 (1 ounce) square unsweetened or
   semisweet chocolate
½ cup butter
¾ cup sugar
1 teaspoon vanilla extract

2 eggs
Prepared graham cracker crust
Whipped topping
Chocolate shavings

Melt chocolate in glass container in microwave on 100 percent power for 1 minute or until melted completely. Stir and cool completely. In bowl, cream butter with sugar. Add melted chocolate and vanilla, scraping bowl at least once with spatula to make sure mixture is well blended. Drop in 1 egg and beat until mixture is fluffy and smooth. Add second egg and repeat. Mixture should be light in color. Pour into graham cracker crust and top with whipped topping and chocolate shavings. Chill at least 4 hours or overnight before serving.

Yield: 8 servings

Chocolate Bar Almond Pie

1 (16 ounce) container nondairy
   whipped topping
3 (7 ounce) chocolate bars with
   almonds

1 cup miniature marshmallows
2 (9 inch) graham cracker crusts

Allow whipped topping to sit at room temperature for 30 minutes, then put into a mixing bowl; set aside. Melt candy bars and marshmallows in double boiler until melted and smooth. Cool slightly. Slowly fold melted chocolate into whipped topping so whipped topping stays fluffy. Pour equal portions into crusts. Refrigerate several hours or overnight.

Yield: 8 slices per pie

Mama's Easy Chocolate Chip Pie

½ cup all-purpose flour
1 cup sugar
2 eggs, beaten
½ cup butter

1 cup nuts
1 cup semisweet chocolate chips
1 teaspoon vanilla extract
Unbaked pie shell

In large bowl, mix flour and sugar well. Add eggs. Stir until well blended. Add butter, nuts, chocolate chips, and vanilla. Pour into unbaked pie shell. Bake at 350 degrees for 40 minutes. Let pie cool completely before cutting.

Yield: 8 servings

Chocolate-Pecan Tassies

Pastry Shell Ingredients:

⅓ cup butter, softened

1 (3 ounce) package cream cheese, softened

¾ cup all-purpose flour

3 tablespoons cocoa powder

2½ tablespoons powdered sugar

Filling Ingredients:

2 large eggs, lightly beaten

⅔ cup sugar

½ cup light corn syrup

2 tablespoons plus 2 teaspoons butter, melted

¾ teaspoon vanilla extract

¾ cup finely chopped pecans

⅓ cup semisweet chocolate mini-morsels

Cream butter and cream cheese for pastry with electric mixer at medium speed; set aside. In another bowl, combine flour, cocoa, and powdered sugar. Mix well. Gradually add flour mixture to creamed mixture. Beat well. Wrap dough in waxed paper and chill 2 hours. Divide dough into 24 balls. Place in lightly greased 1¾-inch miniature muffin pans, pressing dough around edges to make shells. Prick bottom of each shell with a fork; cover and chill at least 1 hour. In large bowl, combine eggs, sugar, corn syrup, butter, and vanilla. Stir well. Add pecans and mini-morsels. Pour mixture into pastry shells and bake at 350 degrees for 30 minutes or until set.

Yield: 24 servings

Coco-nutty Chocolate Pie

4 (1 ounce) squares semisweet
  chocolate
1 cup butter
2 cups sugar
½ cup light corn syrup

¼ teaspoon salt
6 large eggs, lightly beaten
1 teaspoon vanilla extract
1 (7 ounce) can flaked coconut
2 (9 inch) piecrusts

In medium saucepan, heat chocolate and butter over low heat until chocolate melts. Stir often. Remove from heat. Add sugar, corn syrup, and salt. Stir well. Let cool slightly. Stir in eggs, vanilla, and coconut. Pour into piecrusts. Bake at 350 degrees for 35 minutes or just until set. Do not overbake.

Yield: 8 servings per pie

Kathy's Jersey Pie

1 cup sugar
½ cup all-purpose flour
2 eggs, beaten
½ cup butter, softened

1 cup pecans
1 cup semisweet chocolate chips
1 teaspoon vanilla extract
1 (8 inch) piecrust

In large bowl, combine sugar, flour, eggs, and butter. Mix well. Add pecans, chocolate chips, and vanilla. Pour into unbaked piecrust. Bake for 30 minutes at 350 degrees.

Yield: 8 servings

Fudge Pecan Pie

½ cup butter
2 (1 ounce) squares semisweet
 chocolate
1⅛ cups sugar

4 eggs
1 (9 inch) piecrust
1 to 1½ cups chopped pecans

Melt butter and chocolate together in saucepan; beat until smooth. Add sugar and stir. Add eggs, one at a time, beating well after each. Pour into piecrust. Sprinkle with pecans. Bake at 375 degrees for 30 to 35 minutes.

Yield: 8 servings

Double-Chocolate Holiday Pie

4 ounces cream cheese, softened
1 tablespoon sugar
1 tablespoon cold milk
1 (8 ounce) container nondairy
   whipped topping, thawed, divided

1 chocolate graham cracker piecrust
1 (3.4 ounce) box instant chocolate
   pudding
2 cups cold milk

In bowl, mix together cream cheese, sugar, and 1 tablespoon milk until smooth.
Gently stir in 1½ cups nondairy whipped topping. Spread on bottom of
graham cracker crust. In second bowl, stir pudding mix into 2 cups milk until
thick. Immediately stir in remaining whipped topping. Spread over cream
cheese layer. Refrigerate for 4 hours.

Yield: 8 servings

Toffee Ice-Cream Pie & Sauce

Pie Ingredients:
18 vanilla wafers
½ gallon vanilla ice cream

1 cup chopped toffee-chocolate candy
bars, divided

Sauce Ingredients:
1½ cups sugar
1 cup evaporated milk
¼ cup butter

¼ cup light corn syrup
Dash salt

Line bottom and sides of buttered 9-inch pie pan with vanilla wafers. Spoon half of ice cream into wafer shell. Sprinkle with ⅓ cup of the chopped toffee bars. Spoon in remaining ice cream and sprinkle with half the remaining chopped toffee bars. Store pie in freezer until serving time. Prepare sauce by combining sugar, evaporated milk, butter, corn syrup, and salt in large saucepan. Bring to a boil over low heat and stir in remaining chopped toffee. Cool, stirring occasionally. Makes 2½ cups sauce. Drizzle over individual slices of pie just before serving. Pouring sauce over entire pie will make it soggy.

Yield: 8 servings

Granny's German Chocolate Pie

¼ cup butter
4 (1 ounce) squares sweet baking chocolate
1 (1 ounce) can evaporated milk
3 tablespoons cornstarch
1½ cups sugar
⅛ teaspoon salt

2 eggs
1 teaspoon vanilla extract
1 (10 inch) refrigerated piecrust
⅔ cup flaked coconut
⅓ cup chopped pecans
Whipped topping
Chocolate shavings

In saucepan, melt butter and chocolate over medium heat, stirring until chocolate melts. Remove from heat and add evaporated milk. Stir and set aside. Combine cornstarch, sugar, and salt in large bowl. Add eggs and vanilla. Stir well. Gradually add chocolate mixture and stir with wire whisk. Pour mixture into piecrust and sprinkle with coconut and chopped pecans. Bake at 375 for 45 minutes. Cool at least 4 hours. Top with whipped topping and chocolate shavings.

Yield: 8 servings

Heavenly Chocolate Cloud Pie

3 egg whites
1 teaspoon vanilla extract
1 teaspoon baking powder
¾ cup sugar
4 (1 ounce) squares sweet baking chocolate, grated

1 cup buttery round cracker crumbs
½ cup chopped pecans
1 cup whipping cream
2 tablespoons sugar
1 teaspoon vanilla

Beat egg whites and vanilla to soft peaks. In separate bowl, combine baking powder and sugar and gradually add to egg whites, beating until stiff peaks form. Combine all but 2 tablespoons of the grated chocolate with the cracker crumbs. Add crumbs and pecans to egg whites. Spread in 9-inch pie plate. Bake at 350 degrees for 25 minutes. Cool thoroughly. Whip cream with sugar and vanilla and spread onto top of pie. Garnish with remaining chocolate. Refrigerate at least 8 hours.

Yield: 8 servings

Cookies & Brownies & Scones

Like snowflakes, my Christmas memories gather and dance—each beautiful, unique, and too soon gone.

DEBORAH WHIPP

Perfect Holiday Fudge Brownies

Brownie Ingredients:

1 cup butter or margarine

4 (1 ounce) squares unsweetened chocolate

1½ cups plus 2 tablespoons sifted all-purpose flour

½ teaspoon baking powder

1 teaspoon salt

2 cups sugar

4 eggs, slightly beaten

1 teaspoon vanilla extract

¾ cup chopped nuts

Frosting Ingredients:

2 (1 ounce) squares unsweetened chocolate

3 tablespoons butter

5 tablespoons milk

Dash salt

½ teaspoon vanilla extract

2 cups sifted powdered sugar

Melt butter and chocolate in saucepan over very low heat; set aside to cool. In bowl, sift together flour, baking powder, and salt; set aside. In another bowl, gradually add sugar to eggs, mixing thoroughly. Add vanilla and cooled chocolate mixture, blending well. Stir in dry ingredients. Blend in nuts. Bake in greased 13 x 9-inch pan at 375 degrees for 30 to 35 minutes or until wooden pick inserted in center comes out clean. Cool thoroughly. To prepare frosting, combine chocolate, butter, and milk in top of double boiler. Cook over hot water until chocolate and butter melt. Stir to blend thoroughly. Add salt and vanilla. Mix well. Remove from heat. Stir in enough powdered sugar to make mixture of the right consistency for spreading. Frost brownies and cut into squares.

Yield: Approximately 16 servings

Mini Holiday Tuxedo Brownies

1 (19.9 ounce) box fudge brownie mix
48 cupcake wrappers
2 (1 ounce) squares white chocolate
    for baking
2 tablespoons milk
1 (8 ounce) package cream cheese

¼ cup powdered sugar
1 cup thawed, frozen whipped topping
48 maraschino cherries
Melted semisweet chocolate, for
    drizzling

Prepare brownie mix as directed for cakelike brownies. Place cupcake wrappers in muffin pan and fill each ⅔ full. Bake at 325 degrees for 12 to 14 minutes or until edges are set. Do not overbake. Use thumb or (greased) back of measuring spoon to make indentations. Cool in pan 15 minutes. Loosen edges and gently remove brownies from pan. Cool completely. Microwave white chocolate and milk, uncovered, on high for 1 minute; stir until smooth. Cool slightly. In separate bowl, combine cream cheese and powdered sugar; mix well. Gradually stir in white chocolate mixture until smooth. Fold in whipped topping. Put mixture into indentations on cooled brownie cups. Place cherries on top. Drizzle with melted chocolate. Place in airtight container and refrigerate for 1 to 3 hours before serving.

Yield: 4 dozen

Heavenly Cream Cheese–Chocolate Chip Bars

2 packages break-and-bake chocolate
   chip cookie dough
2 (8 ounce) packages cream cheese

¾ cup sugar
3 eggs

Using 1½ packages of cookie dough, break apart and cover bottom of 9 x 13-inch pan. Cream together cream cheese, sugar, and eggs, then pour over cookie mixture. Use remainder of cookie dough and drop evenly onto top of mixture. Bake at 350 degrees for about 30 to 40 minutes.

Yield: 16 servings

Christmas Morning Chocolate Chip Scones

1¾ cups all-purpose flour
3 tablespoons sugar
2½ teaspoons baking powder
½ teaspoon salt
⅓ cup butter

1 egg, slightly beaten
½ cup semisweet chocolate chips
4 to 6 tablespoons half-and-half
1 egg, slightly beaten

In medium bowl, combine flour, sugar, baking powder, and salt. Cut butter into flour mixture until it resembles fine crumbs. Stir in 1 egg, chocolate chips, and just enough half-and-half so dough leaves side of bowl. Turn dough onto lightly floured surface; knead gently 10 times. Roll into ½-inch thick circle; cut into 12 wedges. Place on ungreased cookie sheet. Brush with remaining egg. Bake at 400 degrees for 10 to 12 minutes or until golden brown. Immediately remove from cookie sheet. Serve warm.

Yield: 12 scones

Five-Star Chocolate Christmas Scones

2 cups all-purpose flour
¾ cup sugar
¼ cup Dutch process cocoa powder
2 teaspoons baking powder
½ teaspoon salt
½ cup cold butter, cut into pieces

1 cup whipping cream
1 (1 ounce) square semisweet
   chocolate, melted
1 teaspoon vanilla extract
1 tablespoon whipping cream or milk
2 tablespoons turbinado sugar

In large bowl, combine first 5 ingredients. Cut butter into flour with pastry blender until crumbly. Add 1 cup whipping cream, melted chocolate, and vanilla, stirring with a fork until dry ingredients are moistened. Knead dough in bowl 3 or 4 times. Pat dough into 8-inch circle on lightly greased baking sheet. Cut into 8 wedges using a sharp knife. (Do not separate wedges.) Brush with remaining whipping cream, and sprinkle with turbinado sugar. Bake at 425 degrees for 19 to 20 minutes or until done. Do not overbake.

Yield: 8 scones

Isabella's Heavenly Oatmeal–Chocolate Chip Cookies

1¼ cups butter, softened
¾ cup brown sugar, firmly packed
½ cup sugar
1 egg
1 teaspoon vanilla extract
1½ cups all-purpose flour

1 teaspoon baking soda
½ teaspoon salt (optional)
1 teaspoon ground cinnamon
¼ teaspoon ground nutmeg
3 cups oats (quick or old-fashioned)

In large bowl, beat butter and sugars until creamy. Beat in egg and vanilla. In another bowl, combine flour, baking soda, salt, and spices and add to sugar mixture; mix well. Stir in oats. Drop by rounded tablespoons onto ungreased cookie sheet. Bake at 375 degrees for 8 to 9 minutes for a chewy cookie, 10 to 11 minutes for a crisp cookie. Cool 1 minute on cookie sheet before removing to wire rack.

Yield: 4½ dozen

Chocolate–Cranberry–Macadamia Nut Cookies

1 (18 ounce) roll refrigerated white
    chocolate–chunk cookie dough
1 cup chopped macadamia nuts

1 cup dried, sweetened cranberries
2 teaspoons vanilla extract
1 teaspoon orange extract

In large bowl, crumble cookie dough. Add macadamia nuts, cranberries, and
both extracts. Mix well with electric mixer. Spoon cookie dough by spoonfuls
onto ungreased cookie sheet. Bake at 350 degrees for 12 to 14 minutes or until
golden brown. Remove and let cool.

Yield: 2½ dozen

White Chocolate–Cinnamon Triangles

Cookie Ingredients:

1 (18 ounce) roll refrigerated white chocolate–chunk cookie dough

½ cup honey-roasted cashews or peanuts, chopped

½ cup toffee bits

1 teaspoon cinnamon

Glaze Ingredients:

½ cup powdered sugar

¼ teaspoon cinnamon

2½ to 3 teaspoons milk

In large bowl, break up cookie dough. Add remaining cookie ingredients and mix well. Press dough in bottom of ungreased 9-inch square pan. Bake at 350 degrees for 23 to 27 minutes or until golden brown. Cool 30 minutes. To prepare glaze, blend all ingredients in small bowl until smooth, adding enough milk for desired drizzling consistency. Drizzle over bars. Cool an additional 45 minutes or until completely cooled. Cut into 16 bars. Cut each bar in half diagonally to make triangles.

Yield: 32 bars

Walnut Chocolate Caramel Bars

2 cups all-purpose flour
2 cups old-fashioned oats
1 cup brown sugar, packed
1 teaspoon baking soda
¼ teaspoon salt

1 cup butter or margarine, melted
2 cups semisweet chocolate chips
1½ cups walnuts
1 cup caramel topping mixed with ⅓
cup all-purpose flour

Combine flour, oats, sugar, baking soda, and salt. Add butter. Stir until thoroughly moistened. Reserve 1 cup of mixture and set aside. Press remaining mixure into bottom of ungreased 13 x 9-inch pan. Bake at 350 degrees for 15 minutes until lightly browned. Remove from oven and sprinkle with chocolate chips and walnuts. Drizzle or spread caramel mixture over the top. Sprinkle remaining 1 cup of crumb mixture over all. Bake at 350 degrees for 20 to 25 minutes until browned. Cool in pan.

Yield: 24 bars

Snowball Sandwich Treats

6 ounces white chocolate, chopped

2 (12 ounce) boxes Danish wedding cookies

Melt white chocolate in heavy saucepan over low heat, stirring occasionally. Dip flat sides of half the cookies in white chocolate, and top with the flat sides of remaining cookies. Let stand until white chocolate is firm.

Yield: Approximately 4 dozen

Holiday Peanut Butter–Chocolate Crispy Treats

1½ cups chunky peanut butter
1½ cups light corn syrup
1½ cups sugar

6 cups crisp rice cereal
2 cups semisweet chocolate chips

In large saucepan, heat peanut butter, syrup, and sugar over medium-low heat, stirring constantly, until blended and mixture begins to bubble. Remove from heat. Mix together cereal and chocolate chips in large bowl. Stir in peanut butter mixture until combined. Spread mixture into 13 x 9-inch pan lined with plastic wrap. Cool completely. Lift out of pan and cut into stars or other shapes using 2-inch cookie cutters.

Yield: 22 servings

Angel Kisses

Cookie Ingredients:

¼ cup butter, softened

½ cup brown sugar, packed

2 teaspoons vanilla extract

2 ounces dark chocolate baking bar, melted and cooled

¾ cup all-purpose flour

¼ teaspoon baking soda

⅛ teaspoon salt

Chocolate-Hazelnut Mousse Ingredients:

3 tablespoons butter, softened

⅓ cup chocolate-hazelnut spread

1 cup powdered sugar

2 tablespoons milk

72 toasted hazelnuts

In large bowl, cream butter and brown sugar. Add vanilla and melted chocolate, beating until combined. In small bowl, whisk together flour, baking soda, and salt. Gradually add flour mixture to butter mixture. Shape dough into two 1-inch logs, wrap in plastic wrap, and freeze for 30 minutes or until logs are firm enough to slice. Line large cookie sheet with parchment paper. Unwrap logs and cut into ¼-inch slices. Place slices 1 inch apart and bake at 375 degrees for about 6 minutes or until edges are set. Cool completely. In medium bowl, beat butter and chocolate-hazelnut spread together. Gradually beat in sugar until smooth. Add milk until mixture reaches piping consistency. Using a star tip, pipe small amount of mousse mixture onto each cookie. Top with toasted hazelnut.

Yield: 72 cookies

Peppermint Fudge Brownies

1 cup butter
4 (1 ounce) squares unsweetened chocolate
4 large eggs
2 cups sugar
1½ cups all-purpose flour

½ teaspoon salt
1 tablespoon vanilla extract
½ cup coarsely crushed hard peppermint candies (approximately 20)
2 teaspoons powdered sugar

In heavy saucepan, heat butter and chocolate over medium-low heat, stirring until smooth. Let cool. In bowl, beat eggs at medium speed with electric mixer 2 minutes. Gradually add sugar, beating well. Add melted chocolate mixture, flour, salt, and vanilla. Beat well. Stir in crushed peppermint candies. Pour batter into greased and floured 13 x 9-inch pan. Bake at 350 degrees for 30 to 35 minutes. Cool completely on wire rack. Cut into bars. Sprinkle with powdered sugar.

Yield: 2 dozen

Chocolate-Cherry Oatmeal Cookies

1 cup butter, softened
1 cup brown sugar, packed
¾ cup sugar
2 large eggs
1 tablespoon vanilla extract
2 cups all-purpose flour
2 teaspoons baking powder

½ teaspoon baking soda
½ teaspoon salt
2 cups regular oats
2 (6 ounce) packages white chocolate
    baking bars, coarsely chopped
1 cup sweetened, dried cherries

In large bowl, cream butter at medium speed until fluffy. Gradually add sugars, beating well. Add eggs and vanilla; beat well. In another bowl combine flour, baking powder, baking soda, and salt. Gradually add to butter mixture, beating well. Stir in oats, white chocolate, and cherries. Drop dough using a 1 tablespoon cookie scoop. Bake at 375 degrees for 10 minutes or until lightly browned. Cool 2 minutes before removing to wire racks.

Yield: 5 dozen

Christmas Candy Fudge Bars

2 cups quick oats
1½ cups all-purpose flour
1 cup chopped nuts
1 cup light brown sugar, firmly packed
1 teaspoon baking soda
¼ teaspoon salt

1 cup butter or margarine, melted
1½ cups red and green candy-coated
  chocolate pieces, divided
1 (14 ounce) can sweetened
  condensed milk

Mix together quick oats, flour, nuts, sugar, soda, and salt. Add butter and stir or beat at low speed with an electric mixture until mixture is crumbly. Reserve 1½ cups crumb mixture. Press remaining crumb mixture into lightly greased 13 x 9-inch pan. Bake at 375 degrees for 10 minutes. Cool on wire rack. Reduce oven temperature to 350 degrees. Place 1 cup candy-coated chocolate pieces in microwave-safe bowl. Microwave on high for 1 to 1½ minutes, stirring after 30 seconds. Press chocolate pieces with back of a spoon to mash them. (Candies will be almost melted with pieces of color coating still visible.) Stir in sweetened condensed milk. Spread mixture evenly over crust in pan, leaving ½-inch border on all sides. Combine reserved 1½ cups crumb mixture and remaining ½ cup chocolate pieces. Sprinkle evenly over chocolate mixture, and press lightly. Bake at 350 degrees for 25 to 28 minutes or until golden. Cool in pan on wire rack. Cut into bars.

Yield: 2 dozen

Chocolate Spice Crackles

1 (18.25 ounce) box devil's food cake
    mix
⅓ cup vegetable oil
2 eggs
1 tablespoon ground ginger

½ teaspoon ground pepper
1 tablespoon water
½ cup semisweet chocolate mini-
    morsels
¼ cup sugar

Combine cake mix, oil, eggs, ginger, pepper, and water in large bowl, stirring until smooth. Stir in mini-morsels. Form dough into 1-inch balls. Roll in sugar to coat, and place balls 2 inches apart on lightly greased baking sheets. Bake at 375 degrees for 9 minutes. Cool 2 to 3 minutes before transferring to wire racks.

Yield: 4 dozen

Chocolate Caramel Nut Cookies

1 cup butter, softened
1 cup sugar
1 cup light brown sugar, packed
2 large eggs
1 teaspoon vanilla extract
2 cups all-purpose flour
1 teaspoon baking powder
½ teaspoon baking soda

½ teaspoon salt
2½ cups regular oats
3 (1.91 ounce) packages chocolate-
covered caramel candies, chilled and
chopped
2 (4 ounce) bars white chocolate,
chopped
1½ cups unsalted peanuts, chopped

Cream butter with electric mixer at medium speed. Add sugars and beat well. Add eggs and vanilla, beating until blended. In separate bowl, combine flour, baking powder, baking soda, and salt. In blender or food processor, finely grind oats. Add to flour mixture. Add to butter mixture, beating well. Stir in chopped candy, white chocolate, and peanuts. Form dough into 1½-inch balls, and place on parchment paper–lined cookie sheets. Bake at 375 degrees for 10 minutes or until lightly browned. Remove from oven and allow to cool 1 minute before removing to wire racks.

Yield: 6 dozen

Christmas Shortbread Cookies

1 cup butter, softened
½ cup sugar
¼ teaspoon vanilla extract
2¼ cups all-purpose flour

⅛ teaspoon salt
14 chocolate sandwich cookies,
   coarsely crumbled

Cream butter with electric mixer. Add sugar, beating well. Fold in vanilla. In separate bowl, combine flour and salt. Gradually add to butter mixture, beating at low speed until blended. Stir in cookie crumbs. Roll dough to 1½-inch thickness on lightly floured surface. Cut with 2½-inch round cookie cutter. Place 2 inches apart on ungreased baking sheets. Bake at 275 degrees for 48 minutes or until bottoms are barely brown. Cool 2 minutes before removing to wire racks.

Yield: 1½ dozen

Chocolate Dreams

2 cups sugar
¼ cup cocoa powder
Dash salt
½ cup butter

½ cup milk
3 cups quick oats
1 cup nuts
1 teaspoon vanilla extract

Mix sugar, cocoa, salt, butter, and milk in 3-quart saucepan and bring to a rolling boil. Add oats, nuts, and vanilla. Stir well. Drop by rounded spoonfuls onto waxed paper. Cool.

Yield: 5 dozen

Holiday No-Bake Fudge Cookies

2 cups sugar
½ cup milk
1 teaspoon vanilla extract
½ cup instant chocolate

½ cup butter
3 cups oats
1 cup coconut

Bring sugar, milk, vanilla, chocolate, and butter to a rolling boil, and boil for 1 minute. Combine oats and coconut in large bowl, and add the boiling mixture. Drop by spoonfuls onto waxed paper. Flatten slightly with back of spoon dampened with water. Let set until firm. Store in airtight container.

Yield: 3 dozen

Elaine's Coffee-Flavored Chocolate Chip Biscotti

1 cup sugar
2 cups all-purpose flour
¼ cup Swiss-style coffee drink mix
⅛ teaspoon salt
1 teaspoon baking powder
1 teaspoon baking soda
1 egg
2 egg whites

1 teaspoon vanilla extract
1½ cups semisweet chocolate chips, divided
2 (2 ounce) squares vanilla candy coating
½ cup finely chopped chocolate-covered espresso beans

In large bowl, combine sugar, flour, drink mix, salt, baking powder, and baking soda. In separate bowl, combine egg, egg whites, and vanilla. Blend well. Add egg mixture to dry mixture. Stir well. Add ½ cup chips. Knead mixture on unfloured surface. Form 14 x 4-inch log on lightly greased baking sheet. Bake at 350 degrees for 30 minutes. Cool for 10 minutes. Cut log diagonally into ¾-inch thick slices with a serrated knife. Place slices on ungreased baking sheets and bake for 5 minutes. Turn over and bake another 5 minutes. Cool completely. Microwave candy coating squares in 11 x 7-inch baking dish on high for 1 minute. Stir. Microwave remaining 1 cup chips on high for 30 seconds. Stir well. Dip 1 long side of each biscotti into chocolate mixture. Sprinkle with espresso beans. Let harden.

Yield: 1½ dozen

Christmas Caramelitas

50 caramels
½ cup evaporated milk
2 cups all-purpose flour
2 cups oats
1½ cups brown sugar, packed
1 teaspoon baking soda

½ teaspoon salt
1 cup butter, melted
1 (6 ounce) package semisweet
  chocolate chips
1 cup chopped pecans

Combine caramels and milk in heavy saucepan. Stir until melted. Cool slightly; set aside. In large bowl, combine flour, oats, sugar, baking soda, salt, and butter until crumbly. Press half the crumbs into greased 13 x 9-inch pan. Bake at 350 degrees for 10 minutes. Sprinkle with chocolate chips. Carefully spread with caramel mixture. Press remaining crumbs on top. Bake 15 to 20 minutes longer. Chill 2 hours before serving.

Yield: 48 bars

Forgotten Christmas Cookies

2 egg whites
⅔ cup sugar

½ cup nuts
½ cup mini semisweet chocolate chips

Beat 2 egg whites until stiff. Add sugar slowly. Stir in nuts and chocolate chips. Drop by spoonfuls onto foil. Mixture will puff very little. Place close together. Preheat oven to 350 degrees. Place cookies in oven and turn oven off. Leave cookies in oven overnight.

Yield: 1 dozen

Chocolate Oatmeal Cookies

2½ cups oats
1 cup coconut
½ cup nuts or ¼ cup peanut butter
2 cups sugar

6 tablespoons cocoa powder
½ cup butter
½ cup milk
1 teaspoon vanilla extract

Put oats, coconut, and nuts in bowl and set aside. Bring to a boil sugar, cocoa, butter, and milk. Boil 3 minutes. Remove from heat. Add vanilla and oatmeal mixture to hot mixture. Stir well. Drop by spoonful onto waxed paper and let cool.

Yield: 2 dozen

Candies & Treats

A chocolate in the mouth
is worth two on the plate.

UNKNOWN

Holiday Fudge Royal

3 cups sugar
½ cup cocoa powder
1 cup milk

1 teaspoon vanilla extract
3 tablespoon margarine
1 cup chopped nuts (optional)

Combine sugar and cocoa in saucepan. Add milk; stir over low heat until sugar dissolves. Bring to a boil. Stir occasionally and cook to 236 degrees or until soft-ball stage. Remove from heat. Add vanilla and margarine. Do not stir. Let cool for 15 minutes, then beat until mixture thickens. Add nuts (optional). Pour into buttered dish.

Yield: 24 servings

White Chocolate Lace Stars

1 (24 ounce) package vanilla candy
   coating
1 heavy-duty ziplock bag

Waxed paper
Clear food-safe cello bags

Place candy coating in large heavy-duty ziplock bag and seal. Microwave on medium (50% power) 3 to 4 minutes or until melted. Draw or trace 3- or 4-inch stars on several sheets of waxed paper. Turn paper over, and place on baking sheets. Drizzle candy coating over outline of stars on waxed paper in a lacy design to fill each star. Let harden slightly, then add another layer. Chill at least 15 minutes until hardened. Carefully peel hardened stars from waxed paper, and turn over. Place cookies in cello bags.

Yield: 20 stars

Easy Christmas Turtles

1 (9.1 ounce) package small regular-shaped pretzels (waffle squares or rounds)

1 (13 ounce) package unwrapped caramel-and-chocolate candies (around 60)

1 (6 ounce) package pecan halves or almonds (toasted)

Cover a cookie sheet with aluminum foil and place pretzels individually to form one layer only. Place one caramel-and-chocolate candy on top of each pretzel. Bake at 250 degrees for 4 minutes or until candies are softened. Immediately remove from oven, and quickly place a pecan half on top of each candy, pressing the chocolate into the pretzel to flatten. Cool for 20 minutes, then place uncovered in refrigerator for about 20 minutes to set.

Yield: Approximately 60

Santa's Favorite Fudge

¾ cup butter
3¼ cups sugar
⅔ cup evaporated milk

1 (12 ounce) package semisweet
    chocolate chips
1 (7 ounce) jar marshmallow crème
1 teaspoon vanilla extract
1 cup chopped nuts

Melt first three ingredients in saucepan over medium heat. Using candy thermometer, bring to a boil, stirring constantly, until temperature reaches 234 degrees (about 4 minutes). Add chocolate chips and marshmallow crème, stirring quickly; then add vanilla and nuts. Once combined, pour into foil-lined 13 x 9-inch pan. Cool at room temperature for 4 hours or refrigerate until firm before cutting. To cut, simply use foil to lift fudge from pan.

Yield: 3 pounds

Heavenly Candy Bars

Base Ingredients:
1 cup semisweet chocolate chips
¼ cup creamy peanut butter
¼ cup butterscotch chips

Filling Ingredients:
¼ cup butter
1 cup sugar
¼ cup evaporated milk
1½ cups marshmallow crème
1 cup creamy peanut butter
1 teaspoon vanilla extract
1½ cups chopped salted peanuts

Caramel Ingredients:
1 (14 ounce) package caramels
¼ cup heavy whipping cream

Frosting Ingredients:
1 cup semisweet chocolate chips
¼ cup butterscotch chips
¼ cup peanut butter

Combine *base* ingredients in small saucepan. Stir constantly over low heat until melted and smooth. Spread on bottom of 13 x 9-inch pan; set aside. Melt butter for *filling* in heavy saucepan over medium heat. Stir in sugar and evaporated milk. Bring to a boil and stir for 5 minutes. Remove from heat and stir in marshmallow crème, peanut butter, and vanilla. Add peanuts. Spread over base layer and refrigerate until firm. Combine *caramel* ingredients in saucepan and stir over low heat until melted. Spread over top of filling and refrigerate until smooth. Combine *frosting* ingredients in saucepan and stir over low heat until melted. Pour over caramel layer and refrigerate for at least 1 hour. Cut into squares and store in refrigerator.

Yield: 12 to 24 servings

Holiday Peppermint Bark

1 (12 ounce) package white chocolate chips   24 hard peppermint candies

Line baking sheet with waxed paper. Microwave chips in medium, microwave-safe bowl on 70 percent power for 1 minute; stir. Microwave at additional 10- to 20-second intervals as needed. Stir until smooth. Place peppermint candies in heavy-duty plastic bag and crush with rolling pin. While holding strainer over melted chips, pour crushed candy into strainer. Shake to release all small candy pieces into melted chocolate mixture. Stir, and then spread mixture to desired thickness on baking sheet. Sprinkle with large candy pieces. Press in lightly. Let stand 1 hour or until firm. Break into pieces. Store in airtight container at room temperature.

Yield: Approximately 20 pieces

Christmas Toffee Brickle

40 saltine crackers
1 cup butter
1 cup brown sugar

1 (12 ounce) package semisweet
    chocolate chips
2 cups walnuts or pecans

Wrap cookie sheet with sides in foil. Place crackers, side by side, on sheet. In saucepan, melt butter and mix with brown sugar. Boil 3 to 5 minutes. Pour over crackers. Place in preheated 400-degree oven for about 5 minutes or until bubbly. Remove from oven; then sprinkle on chocolate chips. Put in oven for about 1 minute. Remove, and spread chocolate evenly with flat utensil. Press in nuts. Refrigerate until hard and break into pieces.

Yield: Approximately 40 servings

Mother's Chocolate Bar Toffee

1 cup sugar
1 cup butter
3 tablespoons water

1 teaspoon vanilla extract
3 chocolate bars
¾ cup finely chopped nuts

Cook first 4 ingredients over medium-high heat until medium-dark brown (about 10 to 12 minutes). Mixture will continue to turn brown when taken off heat, so watch that it is not too dark initially. Pour onto buttered 9 x 13-inch pan or buttered heavy-duty foil. Spread quickly. Place chocolate bars on hot toffee; spread when soft. Sprinkle with chopped nuts. Let cool, and break into bite-size pieces.

Yield: Approximately 24 pieces

Easy Holiday Toffee Bars

15 (2½ x 2½-inch) graham crackers
1 cup brown sugar, firmly packed
1 cup butter or margarine

1 cup milk chocolate chips
¼ cup chopped nuts or almonds

Arrange graham crackers so they completely cover bottom of 9 x 13-inch pan, lined with foil and greased with butter or no-stick spray. Mixture medium saucepan, combine brown sugar and butter; bring to a boil. Remove from heat; pour over graham crackers. Bake at 400 degrees for 5 minutes. Remove from oven; immediately sprinkle with chocolate chips. When chips are soft, spread over top; sprinkle with nuts. Chill about 30 minutes until chocolate is set. Cut into bars or break into pieces. Store in refrigerator.

Yield: 24 bars

Holiday Chocolate Peanut Clusters

1 (12 ounce) package semisweet
chocolate chips

1 (6 ounce) package white chocolate
chips

1 teaspoon vanilla extract

1 (7 ounce) can Spanish peanuts

Melt semisweet and white chocolate chips in microwave for 1 minute. Stir;
heat for additional 15 to 30 seconds if necessary. Add vanilla; stir, and add
peanuts. Use a melon scoop or other spoon to drop in clusters onto foil-lined
baking sheet. Refrigerate or freeze until firm. Clusters can be kept at room
temperature once set.

Yield: Approximately 18 to 24

Peppermint-Fudge Truffles

1 cup milk chocolate chips
1 (16 ounce) can chocolate frosting
1½ cups peppermint crunch baking
  chips, divided

½ cup chopped walnuts or pecans
⅛ teaspoon peppermint extract

In microwave-safe bowl, melt milk chocolate chips, stirring until smooth. Stir in frosting, ½ cup peppermint chips, walnuts, and extract. Cover and chill for 30 minutes or until firm enough to form into balls. Coarsely chop remaining peppermint chips. Shape chocolate mixture into 1-inch balls; roll in chopped chips. Store in airtight container in refrigerator.

Yield: 4 dozen

Coco-nutty Candies

2 cups flaked coconut, chopped
3 tablespoons sweetened condensed
  milk
3 tablespoons powdered sugar
2 teaspoons butter, softened

1 (12 ounce) package semisweet
  chocolate chips, divided
8 ounces white candy coating
1 tablespoon shortening
1 (2¼ ounce) package unblanched
  almonds

In large mixing bowl, beat coconut, milk, powdered sugar, and butter until blended, and set aside. In microwave-safe bowl, melt chocolate chips, candy coating, and shortening; stir until smooth. Spoon about ½ teaspoon chocolate mixture into 42 paper-lined miniature muffin cups. Shape ½ teaspoonfuls of coconut mixture into balls; gently press into chocolate. Top each with an almond. Spoon 1 teaspoon chocolate mixture over each. Let stand until set.

Yield: 3½ dozen

Chocolate-Dipped Praline Chews

1 cup light corn syrup
1 cup sugar
⅛ teaspoon salt
¼ cup butter, cubed
2 teaspoons milk

2 cups pecan halves
½ teaspoon vanilla extract
6 ounces white candy coating
6 ounces milk chocolate candy coating

In heavy saucepan, combine corn syrup, sugar, and salt. Bring to a boil over medium heat. Heat to 245 degrees (firm-ball stage), stirring occasionally. Gradually stir in butter, milk, and pecans. Continue cooking until temperature returns to 245 degrees. Remove from heat; stir in vanilla. Immediately drop by teaspoonfuls onto greased baking sheets. Cool. In microwave-safe bowl, melt white chocolate candy coating. Dip candies halfway into coating and allow excess to drip off. Place on waxed paper–lined baking sheets; refrigerate for 15 minutes or until set. Melt milk chocolate coating; dip the other half of each candy and allow excess to drip off. Return to baking sheets and refrigerate until set.

Yield: Approximately 3 dozen

Christmas Caramel-Nut Candy

1½ teaspoons butter
2 (12 ounce) packages milk chocolate chips
¼ cup shortening

1 (14 ounce) package caramels
5 teaspoons water
¼ cup butter, softened
1 cup chopped pecans

Line 13 x 9-inch pan with foil and grease with 1½ teaspoons butter; set aside. Melt chocolate chips and shortening in microwave on 50 percent power for 1 minute; stir until smooth. Spread half of mixture into prepared pan. Refrigerate for 15 minutes or until firm. Set remaining chocolate mixture aside. In another bowl, heat caramels, water, and ¼ cup butter at 70 percent power for 2 minutes; stir. Microwave in additional 10- to 20-second intervals until mixture is melted; stir until smooth. Stir in pecans. Spread over chocolate layer. Heat reserved chocolate mixture, if necessary, to achieve spreading consistency. Spread over caramel layer. Cover and refrigerate for 1 hour or until firm. Using foil, lift candy out of the pan. Gently peel off foil. Cut candy into 1½ x 1-inch bars. Store in refrigerator.

Yield: 2¾ pounds

Triple-Chocolate Christmas Clusters

1 cup milk chocolate chips
1 cup semisweet chocolate chips
2 white chocolate bars

1½ cups pecans
1½ cups broken pretzels

Melt first 3 ingredients in heavy saucepan over low heat, stirring constantly.
Stir in pecans and pretzels. Drop by heaping tablespoons onto lightly greased
waxed paper. Chill in refrigerator at least 1 hour.

Yield: Approximately 3 dozen

Christmas Smoochies

1 (9.1 ounce) bag bite-size, waffle-shaped pretzels

2 (12 ounce) bags chocolate Kisses or similar small candies

1 (16 ounce) bag candy-coated chocolate pieces

Place bite-size, waffle-shaped pretzels (one for each treat) in single layer on cookie sheet lined with parchment paper. Top each pretzel with an unwrapped chocolate Kiss. Bake at 350 degrees for 4 to 6 minutes, until chocolates feel soft when touched with a wooden spoon. Remove cookie sheet from oven and quickly press a chocolate candy into center of each Kiss. Allow treats to cool for a few minutes, then place them in refrigerator to set for about 10 minutes.

Yield: Approximately 30

Old-Fashioned Sour Cream Fudge

2 cups sugar
½ teaspoon salt
1 cup sour cream

2 tablespoons butter
½ cup broken pecans

Combine sugar, salt, and sour cream in saucepan. Cook, stirring occasionally, until a drop in cold water forms a soft ball (236 degrees). Add butter. Let cool to room temperature without stirring. Beat until fudge loses its glossy texture. Add nuts. Pour into 8-inch square pan and let set until firm.

Yield: 24 squares

Christmas Fudge Wreath

1 (12 ounce) package semisweet
  chocolate chips
1 cup butterscotch chips
1 (14 ounce) can sweetened
  condensed milk
1 teaspoon vanilla extract

⅛ teaspoon salt
Butter
1¼ cups candy-coated chocolate
  pieces, divided
½ cup coarsely crushed cream-filled
  chocolate sandwich cookies (about 5)

In heavy, medium-size saucepan, combine chocolate and butterscotch chips and sweetened condensed milk. Reserve condensed milk can. Cook over low heat until melted, stirring often. Remove from heat and stir in vanilla and salt. Cool for about 15 minutes. Grease 8-inch round cake pan with butter and line it with 2 pieces of plastic wrap (overlapping edges, smoothing out any wrinkles). Wrap condensed milk can with aluminum foil, smoothing out wrinkles, and place in center of cake pan. Stir 1 cup candies and crushed cookies into fudge. Spread fudge into cake pan. Sprinkle remaining chocolate candies over fudge, gently pressing candies into fudge. Cover and chill until firm (2 to 3 hours). To remove from cake pan, carefully loosen edges with a sharp knife, and remove can from center. Invert fudge onto plate and then again onto serving platter. Cut into thin slices to serve.

Yield: 2 pounds

Holiday Rocky-Road Granola Clusters

2 tablespoons shortening
1 (16 ounce) package chocolate candy coating, chopped
¼ cup creamy peanut butter
2 to 3 cups coarsely chopped granola bars

¾ cup sesame sticks or thin pretzels
3 teaspoons slivered almonds, toasted
1 cup miniature marshmallows
12 caramels, chopped

In large microwave-safe bowl, combine shortening and chocolate coating. Cover loosely with heavy-duty plastic wrap and microwave on 100 percent power for 1½ minutes or until melted, stirring once. Stir in peanut butter. Let stand 2 minutes. Stir in granola bars, sesame sticks, and almonds. Stir in marshmallows and caramels last so they don't melt. Drop by rounded spoonfuls onto parchment paper. Let clusters stand until firm.

Yield: 2 dozen

Christmas Coffee-Nut Fudge

2 cups sugar
½ cup butter, cut into pieces
2 tablespoons instant coffee granules
⅛ teaspoon salt
1 (5 ounce) can evaporated milk

12 large marshmallows
1 cup semisweet chocolate chips
1 cup chopped pecans or walnuts, toasted
1 teaspoon vanilla extract

In heavy 4-quart saucepan, combine sugar, butter, coffee, salt, evaporated milk, and marshmallows over medium heat, stirring constantly for 10 to 15 minutes or until sugar dissolves and marshmallows are melted. Bring to a boil. Cook, without stirring, to soft-ball stage (234 degrees). Remove from heat. Stir in chocolate chips until melted; add nuts and vanilla, stirring until blended. Spread fudge immediately into 2 aluminum foil–lined, buttered 5¾ x 3½-inch mini loaf pans. Cool completely. Remove from fudge pans. Slice fudge into ½-inch slabs.

Yield: 1½ pounds

Holiday Cracker Candy

2 sleeves buttery rounds (76 crackers),
    broken in half
¾ cup butter
¾ cup light brown sugar, packed

2 cups milk chocolate chips
¾ cup chopped pecans, toasted
½ cup chopped white chocolate

Place crackers on lightly greased aluminum foil–lined jelly-roll pan. Bring butter and brown sugar to a boil in heavy saucepan, stirring constantly. Cook for 3 minutes, stirring often. Pour mixture over crackers. Bake at 350 degrees for 5 minutes. Turn oven off. Sprinkle crackers with chocolate chips. Let stand in oven for 3 minutes or until chocolate melts. Spread melted chocolate evenly over crackers. Top with pecans and white chocolate. Allow to cool completely. Break candy into pieces, and store in refrigerator.

Yield: 2 pounds

Holiday Salted Chocolate Caramels

1 cup semisweet chocolate chips
1 teaspoon shortening

1 (5.5 ounce) package soft and chewy
  rectangular or square caramels,
  unwrapped
⅛ to ¼ teaspoon coarse sea salt

Heat chips and shortening in small, uncovered, microwave-safe bowl on
100 percent power for 1 minute; stir. If necessary, heat at additional 10- to
15-second intervals, stirring until chips are melted. Cool slightly. Dip caramel
pieces (using a fork) into melted chocolate. Shake off excess chocolate and place
on parchment paper–lined cookie sheet. Sprinkle with sea salt. Refrigerate for
15 minutes or until set.

Yield: 20 to 24 caramels

Christmas Walnut Marbled Fudge

1 (12 ounce) package semisweet
  chocolate chips
2 (14 ounce) cans sweetened
  condensed milk, divided

3 cups white chocolate chips
½ teaspoon baking soda, divided
1 cup walnut pieces, divided
½ teaspoon vanilla extract

In medium saucepan, combine semisweet chocolate chips and 1 can condensed milk. In second saucepan, combine white chocolate chips and second can of condensed milk. Add ¼ teaspoon baking soda to each pan. Heat both over medium-low heat until chocolates are melted and smooth (5 to 7 minutes), stirring often. Remove pans from heat and stir ½ cup walnut pieces into each. Add vanilla to semisweet chocolate mixture. Spoon alternate mounds of chocolate mixtures into foil-lined 13 x 9-inch pan. Swirl together with a knife. Refrigerate for 3 hours or until firm. Lift from pan and cut into squares.

Yield: 4 dozen

Crunchy Holiday Fudge with Cookie Twist

2 tablespoons light corn syrup
2 tablespoons butter
¼ teaspoon salt
1 (14 ounce) can sweetened
 condensed milk
1 (18 ounce) roll refrigerated sugar
 cookie dough, cut into small chunks

2 (12 ounce) packages semisweet
 chocolate chips
5 teaspoons vanilla extract
6 (3 pouches from 8.9-ounce box)
 pecan crunchy granola bars, coarsely
 crushed

In heavy 3-quart saucepan, heat corn syrup, butter, salt, and sweetened
condensed milk over medium heat for 2 to 3 minutes, stirring constantly with
wooden spoon until well blended. Reduce heat to medium-low. Stir in cookie
dough chunks. Cook 3 to 5 minutes, stirring constantly, until mixture is smooth
(160 degrees). Remove from heat. Stir in chocolate chips and vanilla until chips
are melted and mixture is smooth. Add crushed granola bars; stir until well
blended. Cook over low heat 1 to 2 minutes, stirring constantly, until mixture
is shiny. Spread into ungreased 13 x 9-inch pan. Refrigerate, uncovered, at least
2 hours. Cut into small squares and serve in decorative candy cups or mini
baking cups.

Yield: 48 candies

Chocolate–Peanut Butter Crunch Cups

1 (18 ounce) roll refrigerated peanut
   butter cookie dough
1 cup white chocolate chips
1½ cups creamy peanut butter, divided

1 cup semisweet chocolate chips
4 (2 pouches from 8.9-ounce box) oats
   and honey crunchy granola bars,
   crushed

Cut cookie dough into 24 slices and press each slice into greased mini-muffin pan. Form ¼-inch rim above top of each muffin cup. Dust fingers with flour if necessary. Bake at 350 degrees for 10 to 15 minutes or until edges are deep golden brown. Cool in pans for 5 minutes. Press down center of each cup with the end of a wooden spoon to make room for filling. In 2-quart saucepan, melt white chocolate chips and half of peanut butter over low heat, stirring constantly. Spoon 1 tablespoon of mixture into each dough-lined cup. Refrigerate 10 minutes. In another 2-quart saucepan, melt chocolate chips and remaining peanut butter over low heat, stirring constantly. Spoon 1 tablespoon of chocolate mixture into each cup. Sprinkle with crushed granola bars and refrigerate for 1 hour.

Yield: 24 candies

Mint-Chocolate Squares

First Layer Ingredients:

2 (1 ounce) squares unsweetened
    chocolate

½ cup butter or margarine

2 eggs

1 cup sugar

½ cup all-purpose flour

1 cup pecans, chopped

Second Layer Ingredients:

2 cups powdered sugar

3 tablespoons butter, softened

2 tablespoons whipping cream

¾ teaspoon pure mint or peppermint
    extract

4 drops green food coloring

Third Layer Ingredients:

1½ cups milk chocolate chips

3 tablespoons vegetable shortening

Melt chocolate and butter in 2-cup (microwave-safe) measure at 100 percent power for 1 minute. Set aside to cool. In bowl, beat eggs and sugar until light and thick; stir in flour, pecans, and melted chocolate. Spoon mixture into greased 7 x 11-inch (microwave-safe) baking dish. Microwave on 100 percent power for 5 to 6 minutes; rotate dish twice. Let stand to cool. In another bowl cream together powdered sugar, butter, cream, mint extract, and green food coloring until smooth. Spread evenly over baked layer. Place chocolate and shortening in 1-quart casserole or bowl. Cover with plastic wrap. Microwave on 50 percent power for 2½ to 3 minutes, until most of the chips are shiny and soft. Stir and spread over mint layer. Cover with plastic wrap and chill. Cut into 1-inch squares.

Yield: 24 candies

Double-Dipped Chocolate-Covered Grahams

6 (2 ounce) vanilla candy coating squares, cut into halves

4 (1 ounce) white chocolate baking squares, chopped

4 tablespoons shortening, divided

18 graham crackers

6 (2 ounce) chocolate candy coating squares, cut in half

4 (1 ounce) semisweet chocolate baking squares, chopped

½ cup toffee bits

In microwave-safe bowl, heat vanilla squares, white chocolate squares, and 2 tablespoons shortening on 100 percent power for 1 to 2 minutes (or until soft). Stir until smooth. Break 9 graham crackers in half and dip each one into chocolate mixture until covered entirely. Place on parchment-lined baking sheet. Chill 20 minutes. Repeat procedure with chocolate squares, remaining 2 tablespoons shortening, and remaining graham crackers. Drizzle any remaining semisweet chocolate and white chocolate over dipped grahams. Sprinkle with toffee bits. Chill until firm.

Yield: 3 dozen

Mousse & More

From home to home, and heart to
heart, from one place to another.
The warmth and joy of Christmas
brings us closer to each other.

EMILY MATTHEWS

Christmas Eve White Chocolate Mousse

Mousse Ingredients:

1 (12 ounce) package white chocolate chips

1½ teaspoons powdered gelatin

3 tablespoons water

¾ cup pasteurized egg product

1½ cups whipping cream

Ganache Ingredients:

8 ounces bittersweet chocolate

1 cup whipping cream

Fresh berries for garnish (optional)

To prepare mousse, melt white chocolate chips in double boiler. In small bowl, whisk gelatin into 3 tablespoons water, and then whisk mixture into chocolate. Add egg product and stir vigorously. In bowl, whip whipping cream until stiff and fold it into chocolate mixture. Pour mousse mixture into mold or individual custard cups. Chill until firm. Prepare ganache by chopping bittersweet chocolate into small pieces and placing them in medium bowl. Bring whipping cream to a boil and pour it over chopped chocolate. Whisk until all chocolate pieces dissolve. Allow mixture to cool to room temperature. Turn mousse mold out onto plate and pour slightly warm ganache over it. If using custard cups, simply add ganache to top. Garnish with fresh berries.

Yield: 10 to 12 servings

Biscuits and Chocolate Gravy

Ingredients for Biscuits:

1½ cups self-rising flour

8 ounces heavy whipping cream

Melted butter for brushing

Ingredients for Chocolate Gravy:

½ cup sugar

1½ tablespoons all-purpose flour

1½ tablespoons cocoa powder

¼ cup milk

½ cup water

4 tablespoons butter, cubed

1 teaspoon pure vanilla extract

Combine flour and cream in large bowl. Stir until dough is evenly blended. Put on floured board. Roll out and cut biscuits with round biscuit cutter. Bake at 375 degrees for 20 minutes or until golden brown. Brush with melted butter. In small saucepan, whisk together sugar, flour, and cocoa powder. Add milk and water and stir until smooth. Bring to a boil over medium heat, whisking constantly until thick and bubbly (3 to 4 minutes). Remove from heat and stir in butter and vanilla. Cut biscuits in half and set them on a plate. Pour chocolate sauce over them. Serve while hot.

Rich "South of the Border" Hot Chocolate

9 cups milk
½ cup dark brown sugar, packed
2 (3.5 ounce) chocolate candy bars
⅓ cup Dutch process or unsweetened
   cocoa powder

3 tablespoons instant espresso powder
1½ teaspoons ground cinnamon
⅔ cup coffee liqueur (optional)
Sweetened whipped cream, ground
   cinnamon, vanilla beans for garnish

Heat milk, sugar, bars, cocoa, espresso powder, and cinnamon in Dutch oven over medium heat for 10 minutes or until chocolate melts and sugar dissolves, stirring occasionally. Remove from heat and whisk vigorously until hot chocolate is frothy. Immediately pour into mugs. Stir a splash of coffee liqueur into each serving, if desired. Top with whipped cream, and sprinkle with cinnamon or add a vanilla bean to each mug as a stir stick.

Yield: 11 cups

Chocolate Crunch Popcorn

2 cups milk chocolate chips, divided
1½ cups light brown sugar, packed
¾ cup butter
¾ cup light corn syrup
¼ teaspoon salt

1½ teaspoons vanilla extract
¾ teaspoon baking soda
2 (3.5 ounce) bags natural-flavored
   microwave popcorn, popped
2 cups peanuts or cashews

Bring 1 cup chocolate chips, sugar, butter, corn syrup, and salt to a boil in heavy saucepan over medium heat, stirring constantly. Remove from heat and stir in vanilla and baking soda.

Distribute popcorn and nuts evenly into 2 lightly greased roasting pans. Remove all unpopped kernels. Pour chocolate mixture over popcorn and nuts, stirring well with a lightly greased spatula. Bake at 250 degrees for 1 hour, stirring every 15 minutes. Spread on waxed paper to cool, breaking apart large clumps. Sprinkle remaining 1 cup chocolate chips evenly over hot popcorn. Let cool. Store in airtight containers.

Yield: About 29 cups

White Chocolate–Caramel Sauce

1 cup water
2 cups sugar
1 cup heavy whipping cream
⅛ teaspoon salt

1 teaspoon vanilla extract
1 (4 ounce) premium white chocolate
   baking bar, chopped

In heavy saucepan, combine water and sugar. Cover and bring to a boil over high heat. Uncover. Cook to 300 degrees (about 15 minutes). Reduce heat to medium and cook to 350 degrees (about 5 minutes). Meanwhile, bring whipping cream to a simmer in small saucepan. Remove caramel syrup from heat, and carefully add cream to caramel. Mixture will bubble up. Add salt and vanilla. Stir until bubbling begins to subside. Add white chocolate (which will appear to separate). Whisk gently until smooth. Cool to room temperature. Cover and chill up to 1 month. Serve warm.

Yield: 2⅓ cups

Rich Dark Chocolate–Raspberry Fondue

⅔ cup heavy whipping cream
⅓ cup seedless raspberry preserves
1 tablespoon honey

1 (12 ounce) package semisweet
   chocolate chunks
Assorted dippers (fresh fruit,
   shortbread cookies, pound cake or
   angel food cubes, pretzels)

In fondue pot or 2-quart saucepan, mix together cream, raspberry preserves, and honey. Heat over warm/simmer setting or medium-low heat, stirring occasionally, until bubbles rise to the surface. Do not boil. Add chocolate, stirring with wire whisk until melted. Keep warm over warm/simmer setting. Serve with dippers.

Yield: 16 servings

Holiday Pops

20 lollipop sticks
20 large marshmallows
1 cup white chocolate chips

1 cup milk chocolate chips
Decorator icing
Assorted candies and chocolates

Line baking sheet with waxed or parchment paper. Insert lollipop stick halfway through each marshmallow and set aside. Melt white chocolate chips according to package directions. Immediately dip 10 marshmallow pops lightly into melted chips for a thin coating. Place on parchment paper–lined baking sheet. Repeat process with chocolate chips and remaining marshmallows. Refrigerate for 10 minutes or until hardened. Use decorator icing to decorate pops and/or "glue" on candy pieces.

Festive Chocolate-Dipped Pretzels

1 (12 ounce) package white chocolate chips

1 (8 ounce) bag red candy coating melts

1 (12 ounce) package milk chocolate or semisweet chocolate chips

36 pretzel rods

Assorted colored sugars and nonpareils

In microwave-safe glass bowl, heat white chocolate chips at 60 percent power for 1 minute. Stir. Repeat as necessary, stirring until smooth. Place red candy melts in 2 small glass bowls and microwave as with white chocolate. Transfer to a pastry bag, snipping off a small opening at the tip. Repeat heating process with milk/semisweet chocolate, stirring until smooth. Spoon white or milk/semisweet chocolate over ¾ of each pretzel rod. Tap off excess and sprinkle with colored sugar or nonpareils, if desired. Place on waxed paper. Drizzle those left plain with red candy melts using pastry bag.

Yield: 36 pretzels

Yuletide Chocolate Lover's Coffee

4 (1 ounce) squares semisweet
   chocolate, chopped
2 cups half-and-half

4 cups hot brewed coffee
¾ cup coffee liqueur
Whipped topping

In large saucepan, combine chocolate and half-and-half over medium-low heat.
Whisk constantly for 10 minutes or until melted (and smooth). Stir in coffee.
Remove from heat and stir in liqueur. Serve warm with sweetened whipped
topping.

Yield: 7½ cups

Mint-Chocolate Coffee Mix

¼ cup instant coffee granules
¼ cup powdered nondairy coffee
   creamer
⅓ cup sugar

2 tablespoons cocoa
1½ tablespoons crushed hard
   peppermint candies

Place all ingredients in blender and process until well blended. Divide mixture into jars. Add these serving directions to the jar: Combine 2 tablespoons Mint-Chocolate Coffee Mix and ¾ cup boiling water; stir well.

Yield: 8 servings

Minted Hot Chocolate Mix

1 cup powdered nondairy coffee
    creamer
1 cup powdered sugar

½ cup miniature marshmallows
¼ cup cocoa powder
¼ cup mint chocolate chips

Combine all ingredients. Divide mixture into jars. Add these serving directions
to the jar: Combine ⅓ cup Minted Hot Chocolate Mix with ⅔ cup boiling
water; stir well.

Yield: 7 servings

Holiday Party Trash Mix

1 (6 ounce) package semisweet or milk chocolate chips
2 tablespoons cooking oil
1 cup peanut butter

1 box corn, wheat, or rice cereal squares
1 box powdered sugar

In saucepan, heat chocolate chips, oil, and peanut butter until melted. Set aside to cool. In large bowl, mix cereal and cooled chocolate mixture to coat. Add powdered sugar and coat well. Refrigerate until well set.

Yield: 5 to 6 cups

Holiday Gorp

½ cup creamy peanut butter
¼ cup creamy almond butter
1½ cups white chocolate baking chips
¼ cup plus 2 tablespoons butter
1 tablespoon honey
¼ teaspoon ground cinnamon
8 cups crispy corn and rice cereal squares

3 cups pretzel-flavored fish-shaped crackers
1½ cups powdered sugar
2 cups salted, roasted almonds with skins
2 cups red and green candy-coated chocolate pieces
1½ cups sweetened cranberries

In saucepan, combine peanut butter, almond butter, chocolate chips, butter, honey, and cinnamon. Cook over medium heat, stirring until chips and butter melt. Place cereal and crackers in bowl and add melted chocolate mixture. Stir until well coated; let cool slightly. Place powdered sugar in large plastic ziplock bag. Add a portion of the chocolate-coated cereal mixture. Seal and toss until coated. Repeat until the cereal is all sugar coated. Combine cereal mixture, almonds, candy-coated chocolate, and cranberries in large bowl. Stir gently to blend. Store in airtight container.

Yield: 18 cups

Chocolate Potato Chips

2 (12 ounce) packages semisweet or milk chocolate chips
1 tablespoon shortening

1 (16 ounce) bag of ridged potato chips

In heavy saucepan, melt chocolate chips and shortening over low heat. Stir constantly. Using a pastry brush, dip bristles in chocolate and paint one side of each potato chip. Place chip chocolate side up on parchment paper. Allow to cool until set. Refrigeration may cause these to become soggy.

Yield: Approximately 16 servings

Holiday Fudge Waffles à la Mode with Peppermint-Chocolate Sauce

Waffle Ingredients:

2 large eggs
1 teaspoon vanilla extract
¼ cup butter or margarine, melted
1 cup buttermilk
1 cup all-purpose flour
½ teaspoon baking powder
½ teaspoon baking soda
¼ teaspoon salt

¼ teaspoon ground nutmeg
¾ cup sugar
½ cup cocoa powder
½ cup chopped walnuts
¼ cup semisweet chocolate mini-morsels
Vanilla ice cream

Sauce Ingredients:

2 cups semisweet chocolate chips
1¼ to 1½ cups half-and-half, divided

½ cup finely crushed hard peppermint candy

Combine first three ingredients in large mixing bowl. Beat at medium speed with electric mixer until foamy. Add buttermilk, mixing well; set aside. In another bowl combine flour and next 6 ingredients. Gradually add flour mixture to egg mixture, beating at low speed until just blended. Stir in walnuts and mini-morsels. Bake in preheated, oiled waffle iron until golden. To prepare peppermint-chocolate sauce, combine chocolate chips, 1 cup of half-and-half, and crushed candy in small saucepan. Cook over medium-low heat for about 12 minutes or until candy melts, stirring often. Stir in enough remaining half-and-half for desired consistency. Serve waffles with vanilla ice cream and warm peppermint-chocolate sauce.

Yield: 12 (4-inch) waffles

Santa's Hot Fudge Sauce

2 (1 ounce) squares unsweetened
    chocolate
1 (5 ounce) can evaporated milk
½ cup sugar

2 tablespoons unsalted butter
2 tablespoons light corn syrup
1½ teaspoons vanilla extract
⅛ teaspoon salt

Finely chop chocolate and set aside. In small, heavy saucepan, heat evaporated milk and sugar over medium heat, stirring until sugar is dissolved. Add chocolate, butter, and corn syrup to milk mixture and continue to cook, stirring constantly, just until smooth. Bring mixture to a boil over moderate heat, stirring occasionally, and gently boil for 8 minutes. Remove pan from heat and stir in vanilla and salt. Fudge sauce keeps, covered and chilled, for 3 weeks. Cool fudge sauce completely before covering as any condensation will make it grainy. Reheat fudge sauce, uncovered, over simmering water in double boiler.

Yield: 1 cup

Rich & Dreamy Chocolate Dip

8 ounces milk chocolate
½ cup water
2 tablespoons honey
1 teaspoon vanilla extract

2 tablespoons water
½ cup heavy cream
2 tablespoons butter
¼ cup toasted almond slivers

Dissolve chocolate with water in ceramic fondue pot over low flame. Add honey and remaining ingredients in above order and stir well. Let simmer 25 minutes, then transfer to the warmer. Dip works well with strawberries, angel food cake, apples, etc.

Chocolate Plunge

⅔ cup light or dark corn syrup
½ cup heavy whipping cream

1 (8 ounce) package semisweet
    chocolate chips
Assorted fresh fruit

In medium saucepan, combine corn syrup and cream. Bring to a boil over medium heat. Remove from heat. Add chocolate; stir until completely melted. Serve warm as a dip for fruit or cookies.

Microwave Instructions:
In medium microwaveable bowl, combine corn syrup and cream. Microwave on high for 1½ minutes or until boiling. Add chocolate; stir until completely melted.

Yield: 1½ cups

Holiday Chocolate Frosting

2 cups sifted powdered sugar
1 egg
⅓ cup soft margarine

2 (1 ounce) squares unsweetened
chocolate, melted

In bowl, combine all ingredients. Beat until fluffy.

Yield: Approximately 2 cups

Chocolate-Covered Strawberries

15 strawberries, fully ripe but still firm
4 (1 ounce) squares semisweet or milk
chocolate

1 teaspoon shortening

Wash and dry strawberries. Do not remove stems. Place chocolate squares and shortening in heavy saucepan. Stirring constantly, allow chocolate to melt on low heat. Remove from heat and stir until smooth. Holding each strawberry by its stem, dip bottom half into chocolate mixture. Place on parchment paper until chocolate is set. Store in refrigerator.

Yield: 15 servings

Christmas Coffee Punch

3 quarts water
½ cup instant coffee granules
2 cups sugar

1 (6 ounce) can chocolate syrup
3 quarts milk
3 quarts vanilla ice cream

In large saucepan, mix water and coffee and bring to a boil. Add sugar and chocolate syrup. Chill overnight. Add milk and ice cream 30 minutes before serving.

Yield: 24 to 36 servings

Creamy Chocolate Icing

2 cups sugar
¼ cup cocoa powder
½ cup butter

½ cup milk
½ teaspoon vanilla extract

Mix sugar, cocoa, butter, and milk together in saucepan. Cook on high and stir until boiling. Boil for 1 minute. Add vanilla. Pour into mixer and beat on high until creamy and dull, rather than shiny.

Yield: Approximately 2 cups

Notes

Notes

Notes

Notes

Notes

Notes

Notes

Notes

Index

[Mary] brought forth her firstborn son, and wrapped him in swaddling clothes, and laid him in a manger; because there was no room for them in the inn.

LUKE 2:7